Aristophanes, Benjamin Bickley Rogers

The Revolt of the Women

A Free Translation of the Lysistrata of Aristophanes

Aristophanes, Benjamin Bickley Rogers

The Revolt of the Women
A Free Translation of the Lysistrata of Aristophanes

ISBN/EAN: 9783337008611

Printed in Europe, USA, Canada, Australia, Japan

Cover: Foto ©Thomas Meinert / pixelio.de

More available books at **www.hansebooks.com**

THE

REVOLT OF THE WOMEN.

A FREE TRANSLATION

OF THE

LYSISTRATA OF ARISTOPHANES.

(ACTED AT ATHENS, B.C. 411.)

BY

BENJAMIN BICKLEY ROGERS, M.A.

OF LINCOLN'S INN, BARRISTER-AT-LAW ; AND SOMETIME FELLOW OF
WADHAM COLLEGE, OXFORD.

LONDON:

GEORGE BELL & SONS,
YORK STREET, COVENT GARDEN.

LONDON :

GILBERT AND RIVINGTON, PRINTERS,

ST. JOHN'S SQUARE.

NOTICE.

FINDING that I have not at present, and fearing that I may never have, sufficient health and leisure to carry through the Press complete editions of the remaining Plays of Aristophanes, similar to my edition of the Wasps, I propose to print the bare translations, long since finished, without text or commentary.

3, OLD SQUARE, LINCOLN'S INN,
April, 1878.

CHARACTERS OF THE DRAMA.

WOMEN.

LYSISTRATA,
CALONICE,
MYRRHINA,
STRATYLLIS,
} Athenian Women.

LAMPITO, a Spartan Woman.

CHORUS OF WOMEN.

A Bœotian Woman (ISMENIA), a Corinthian Woman, a Scythian Archeress, and several Athenian Women. Also RECONCILIATION, the handmaiden of Lysistrata.

MEN.

AN ATHENIAN MAGISTRATE.

CINESIAS, the husband of Myrrhina.

LACONIAN HERALD.

LACONIAN AMBASSADORS.

ATHENIAN AMBASSADORS.

IDLERS.

A PORTER.

CHORUS OF MEN.

Scythian Archers, and several Athenians and Laconians. Also Myrrhina's child.

THE LYSISTRATA.

It is daybreak at Athens; and Lysistrata, a young and beautiful woman, is standing alone, with marks of evident anxiety in her countenance and demeanour. The scene represents the sloping hill which rises from the Lower to the Upper City. In the background are the Propylæa, the splendid portals of the Athenian Acropolis. Lysistrata is on the look-out for persons who do not come, and after exhibiting various symptoms of impatience, she suddenly begins to speak with abrupt and indignant emphasis.

LYSISTRATA. Now were they summoned to some shrine of Bacchus,
　　　Pan, Colias, Genetyllis,[1] there had been
　　　No room to stir, so thick the crowd of timbrels.
　　　And NOW!—there's not one woman to be seen.
　　　Stay, here comes one, my neighbour Calonice.
　　　Good morning, friend.　　CALONICE. Good morn, Lysistrata.
　　　Why, what's the matter? don't look gloomy, child.
　　　It don't become you to knit-knot your eyebrows.
LYS.　My heart is hot within me, Calonice,
　　　And sore I grieve for sake of womankind,
　　　Because the men account us all to be
　　　Sly, shifty rogues.　　CAL. And so, by Zeus, we are.
LYS.　Yet though I told them to be here betimes,
　　　To talk on weighty business, they don't come,

---

[1] All Gods of Wine and Love, the chief pleasures, according to Aristophanes, of the Athenian women.

They're fast asleep. CAL. They'll come, dear heart, they'll come.
'Tis hard, you know, for women to get out.
One has to mind her husband : one, to rouse
Her servant : one, to put the child to sleep :
One has to wash him : one, to give him pap.

LYS. Ah ! but they've other duties still more pressing
Than such as these. CAL. Well but, Lysistrata,
Why have you, dear, convoked us? Is the matter
A weighty subject? LYS. Weighty? yes. CAL. And pregnant?

LYS. Pregnant, by Zeus. CAL. Why ever don't we come, then?

LYS. No, it's not that : we'd have come fast enough
For such-like nonsense. 'Tis a scheme I've hit on,
Tossing it over many a sleepless night.

CAL. Tossing it over? then 'tis light, I fancy.

LYS. Light? ay, so light, my dear, that all the hopes
Of all the States are anchored on us women.

CAL. Anchored on us! a slender stay to lean on.

LYS. Ay, all depends on us : whether as well the
Peloponnesians all shall cease to be—

CAL. Sure and 'tis better they should cease to be.

LYS. And all the dwellers in Bœotia perish—

CAL. Except the eels ; do pray except the eels.

LYS. But about Athens, mark you, I won't utter
Such words as these : you must supply my meaning.
But if the women will but meet here now,
Bœotian girls, Peloponnesian girls,
And we ourselves, we'll save the States between us.

CAL. What can we women do? What brilliant scheme
Can we, poor souls, accomplish? we who sit
Trimmed and bedizened in our saffron silks,
Our cambric robes, and little finical shoes.

LYS. Why, they're the very things I hope will save us,
Your saffron dresses, and your finical shoes,

Your paints, and perfumes, and your robes of gauze.

CAL. How mean you, save us?   LYS. So that nevermore
Men in our day shall lift the hostile spear—

CAL. O, by the Twain, I'll use the saffron dye.

LYS. Or grasp the shield—   CAL. I'll don the cambric robe.

LYS. Or draw the sword.   CAL. I'll wear the finical shoes.

LYS. Should not the women, then, have come betimes?

CAL. Come? no, by Zeus; they should have flown with wings.

LYS. Ah, friend, you'll find them Attic to the core:
Always too late in everything they do.
Not even one woman from the coast has come,
Not one from Salamis.   CAL. O they, no doubt,
Will cross this morning, early, in their boats.

LYS. And those I counted sure to come the first,
My staunch Acharnian damsels, they're not here—
Not they.   CAL. And yet Theagenes's wife
Consulted Hecate, as if to come.

(Several women enter, headed by Myrrhina, from the village of Anagyrus. Others soon follow.)

Hi! but they're coming now: here they all are:
First one, and then another.   Hoity toity!
Whence come all these?   LYS. From Anagyre.   CAL. Aha!
We've stirred up Anagyre² at all events.

MYRRHINA. Are we too late, Lysistrata?   Well?   What?
Why don't you speak?   LYS. I'm sorry, Myrrhina,
That you should come so late on such a business.

MYRR. I scarce could find my girdle in the dark.
But if the thing's so pressing, tell us now.

LYS. No, no, let's wait a little, till the women
Of Peloponnesus and Bœotia come

---

² To stir up Anagyre (meaning the nauseous-smelling shrub of that name) was
a proverb, used of persons who brought some unpleasantness on themselves.
Calonice applies the proverb to the deme, meaning that the influx of Anagyrasian
women proves that the deme Anagyre was thoroughly stirred up.

To join our congress.   MYRR. O yes, better so.
And here, good chance, is Lampito approaching.

(Lampito, a Spartan woman, enters, accompanied by her friends.)

LYS. O welcome, welcome, Lampito, my love.
O the sweet girl ! how hale and bright she looks !
Here's nerve ! here's muscle ! here's an arm could fairly
Throttle a bull !   LAMPITO. Weel, by the Twa, I think sae.
An' I can loup an' fling an' kick my hurdies.

LYS. See here's a neck and breast; how firm and lusty !

LAMP. Wow, but ye pradd me like a fatted calf.

LYS. And who's this other damsel ? whence comes she ?

LAMP. Ane deputation frae Bœoty, comin'
To sit amang you.   LYS. Ah, from fair Bœotia,
The land of plains !   CAL. A very lovely land,
Well cropped, and trimmed, and spruce with penny-royal.

LYS. And who's the next ?   LAMP. A bonnie burdie she,
She's a Corinthian lassie.   LYS. Ay, by Zeus,
And so she is. A bonnie lass, indeed.

LAMP. But wha ha' ca'ed thegither a' thae thrangs
O' wenches ?   LYS. I did.   LAMP. Did ye noo ? then tell us
What 'tis a' for.   LYS. O yes, my dear, I will.

MYRR. Ay, surely : tell us all this urgent business.

LYS. O yes, I'll tell you now ; but first I'd ask you
One simple question.   MYRR. Ask it, dear, and welcome.

LYS. Do ye not miss the fathers of your babes,
Always on service ? well I wot ye all
Have got a husband absent at the wars.

CAL. Ay, mine, worse luck, has been five months away
In Thracian quarters, watching Eucrates.

MYRR. And mine's been stationed seven whole months at Pylus.

LAMP. An' my gude mon nae suner comes frae war
Than he straps targe an' gangs awa' again.

LYS. No husbands now, no sparks, no anything.

For ever since Miletus played us false,
We've had no joy, no solace, none at all.
So will you, will you, if I find a way,
Help me to end the war?   Myrr. Ay, that we will.
I will, be sure, though I'd to fling me down
This mantling shawl, and have a bout of—drinking.[3]

Cal. And I would cleave my very self in twain
Like a cleft turbot, and give half for Peace.

Lamp. An' I, to glint at Peace again, wad speel
Up to the tap rig o' Taygety.

Lys. I'll tell you now: 'tis meet ye all should know.
O ladies! sisters! if we really mean
To make the men make Peace, there's but one way,
We must abstain— Myrr. Well! tell us. Lys. Will ye do it?

Myrr. Do it? ay, surely, though it cost our lives.

Lys. We must abstain—each—from the joys of Love.
How! what! why turn away? where are ye going?
What makes you pout your lips, and shake your heads?
What brings this falling tear, that changing colour?
Will ye, or will ye not? What mean ye, eh?

Myrr. I'll never do it. Let the war go on.

Cal. Zeus! nor I either. Let the war go on.

Lys. You, too, Miss Turbot? you who said just now
You'd cleave, for Peace, your very self in twain?

Cal. Ask anything but this. Why, if needs be,
I'd walk through fire: only, not give up Love.
There's nothing like it, dear Lysistrata.

Lys. And what say you? Myrr. I'd liefer walk through fire.

Lys. O women! women! O our frail, frail sex!
No wonder tragedies are made from us.

---

[3] 'Fighting' was the word expected; but Aristophanes is, throughout this scene, playing upon the alleged bibulous propensities of Athenian women.

Always the same : nothing but loves and cradles.
O friend ! O Lampito ! if you and I
Are of one mind, we yet may pull things through ;
Won't *you* vote with me, dear ?   Lamp. Haith, by the Twa',
'Tis sair to bide your lane, withouten men.
Still it maun be : we maun hae Peace, at a' risks.

Lys. O dearest friend ; my one true friend of all.

Cal. Well, but suppose we do the things you say,
　Pray Heaven avert it, but put case we do,
　Shall we be nearer Peace ?   Lys. Much, much, much nearer.
　For if we women will but sit at home,
　Powdered and trimmed, clad in our daintiest lawn,
　Employing all our charms, and all our arts
　To win men's love, and when we've won it, then
　Repel them, firmly, till they end the war,
　We'll soon get Peace again, be sure of that.

Lamp. Sae Menelaus, when he glowered, I ween,
At Helen's breastie, coost his glaive awa'.

Cal. Eh, but suppose they leave us altogether?

Lys. O, faddle! then we'll find some substitute.

Cal. If they try force?   Lys. They'll soon get tired of that
If we keep firm.   Scant joy a husband gets
Who finds himself at discord with his wife.

Cal. Well, then, if so you wish it, so we'll have it.

Lamp. An' our gude folk we'se easily persuade
To keep the Peace wi' never a thocht o' guile :
But your Athanian hairumscairum callants
Wha sall persuade them no to play the fule?

Lys. O we'll persuade our people, never fear.

Lamp. Not while ye've gat thae gallies rigged sae trim,
An' a' that rowth o' siller nigh the Goddess.

Lys. O but, my dear, we've taken thought for that :
This very morn we seize the Acropolis.

Now, whilst we're planning and conspiring here,
The elder women have the task assigned them,
Under pretence of sacrifice, to seize it.

LAMP. A' will gae finely, an' ye talk like that.

LYS. Then why not, Lampito, at once combine
All in one oath, and clench the plot securely?

LAMP. Weel, you propound the aith, an' we'se a' tak' it.

LYS. Good; now then, Scythianess, don't stand there gaping.
Quick, set a great black shield here, hollow upwards,
And bring the sacrificial bits. CAL. And how
Are we to swear, Lysistrata? LYS. We'll slay
(Like those Seven Chiefs in Æschylus), a lamb
Over a shield. CAL. Nay, when our object's Peace,
Don't use a shield, Lysistrata, my dear.

LYS. Then what shall be the oath? CAL. Could we not somehow
Get a grey mare, and cut her up to bits?

LYS. Grey mare, indeed! CAL. Well, what's the oath will suit
Us women best? MYRR. I'll tell you what I think.
Let's set a great black CUP here, hollow upwards:
Then for a lamb we'll slay a Thasian wine-jar,
And firmly swear to—pour no water in.

LAMP. Hech, the braw aith! my certie, hoo I like it.

LYS. O yes, bring out the wine-jar and the cup.

(A maiden brings out a jar of wine and an immense cup.)

CAL. La! here's a splendid piece of ware, my dears.
Now that's a cup 'twill cheer one's heart to take.

LYS. *(To the servant.)* Set down the cup, and take the victim boar.[4]
O Queen Persuasion, and O Loving Cup,
Accept our offerings, and maintain our cause!

(The servant pours the wine into the cup, the women all pressing round to see.)

CAL. 'Tis jolly coloured blood, and spirts out bravely!

[4] She means the *Wine-jar*, but she speaks of it as a victim whose blood is about to be shed.

LAMP. Ay, an' by Castor, vera fragrant too!
MYRR. Let *me* swear first, my sisters! CAL. Yes, if *you*
    Draw the first lot; not else, by Aphrodite.
LYS. All place your hands upon the wine-cup: so.
    One, speak the words, repeating after me.
    Then all the rest confirm it. Now begin.

       I will abstain from Love and Love's delights.
CAL. *I will abstain from Love and Love's delights.*
LYS. And take no pleasure though my lord invites.
CAL. *And take no pleasure though my lord invites.*
LYS. And sleep a vestal all alone at nights.
CAL. *And sleep a vestal all alone at nights.*
LYS. And live a stranger to all nuptial rites.
CAL. *And live a stranger to all nuptial rites.*
       I don't half like it though, Lysistrata.
LYS. I will abjure the very name of Love.
CAL. *I will abjure the very name of Love.*
LYS. So help me Zeus, and all the Powers above.
CAL. *So help me Zeus, and all the Powers above.*
LYS. If I do this, my cup be filled with wine.
CAL. *If I do this, my cup be filled with wine.*
LYS. But if I fail, a water draught be mine.
CAL. *But if I fail, a water draught be mine.*

LYS. You all swear this? MYRR. O yes, my dear, we do.
       (Lysistrata takes the wine-cup in her hand.)
LYS. I'll now consume these fragments. CAL. Shares, my friend,
    Now at first starting let us show we're friends.
       (A sound of persons cheering is heard in the distance)
LAMP. Hark! what's yon skirlin'? LYS. That's the thing I said.
    They've seized the Acropolis, Athene's castle,
    Our comrades have. Now, Lampito, be off:
    You, go to Sparta, and arrange things there,

Leaving us here these girls as hostages.
And We will pass inside the castle walls,
And help the women there to close the bars.

CAL. But don't you think that very soon the Men
Will come, in arms, against us ? LYS. Let them come!
They will not bring or threats or fire enough
To awe our woman hearts, and make us open—
These gates again, save on the terms we mentioned

CAL. By Aphrodite, no! else 'twere for nought
That people call us bold, resistless jades.

(The crowd now disperses: Lampito leaving for her homeward journey, and the others dis-
-appearing through the gates of the Propylœa. After a pause the Chorus of Men are seen
slowly approaching from the Lower City. They are carrying heavy logs of firewood, and
a jar of lighted cinders; and as they move, they sing their entrance song.)

CHORUS OF MEN. On, sure and slow, my Draces, go: though that great
    log you're bringing
Of olive green, is sore, I ween, your poor old shoulder wringing.
O dear, how many things in life bely one's expectations!
Since who'd have thought, my Strymodore, that these abomi-
    nations,
    Who would have thought that sluts like these,
    Our household pests, would have waxed so bold,
    As the Holy Image by fraud to seize,
    As the City Castle by force to hold,
    With block and bolt and barrier vast, -
    Making the Propylæa fast.
Press on, Philurgus, towards the heights; we'll pile a great
    amazing
Array of logs around the walls, and set them all a-blazing:
And as for these conspirators, a bonfire huge we'll make them,
One vote shall doom the whole to death, one funeral pyre shall
    take them,
And thus we'll burn the brood accurst, but Lycon's wife we'll
    burn the first.

No, never, never, whilst I live, shall woman-folk deride me :
Not scatheless went Cleomenes,[5] when he like this defied me,
   And dared my castle to seize : yet He,
   A Spartan breathing contempt and pride,
   Full soon surrendered his arms to me,
   And a scanty coat round his loins he tied,
   And with unwashed limbs, and with unkempt head,
   And with six years' dirt, the intruder fled ;
So strict and stern a watch around my mates and I were keeping,
In seventeen rows of serried shields before the fortress sleeping.
And THESE, whom both Euripides and all the Powers on high
Alike detest, shall these, shall these, my manly rage defy ?
Then never be my Trophy shown, on those red plains of
   Marathon !

   But over this snubby protruding steep
   Ere we reach our goal at the Castle keep,
  We've still, with our burdensome load, to creep.
   And how to manage that blunt incline
   Without a donkey, I can't divine.
Dear, how these two great firelogs make my wearied shoulders
   toil and ache.
   But still right onward we needs must go,
   And still the cinders we needs must blow,
Else we'll find the fire extinguished, ere we reach our journey's
   end.
    Puff ! Puff ! Puff ![6]
    O the smoke ! the smoke !

   O royal Heracles ! what a lot
   Of fire came raging out of the pot,
  And flew, like a dog, at my eyes, red hot.

[5] The story is told by Herodotus, V. 72.
[6] Φῦ is not, as the Oxford lexicographers describe it, an exclamation of disgust,

'Twas a jet from the Lemnian mines, I ween,
It came so fierce, and it bit so keen,
And worried, with persistence sore, my two poor eyes, inflamed
before.
On, Laches, on! to the castle press,
And aid the God in her dire distress;
Surely, if we e'er would help her, now's the very time, my friend.
Puff! Puff! Puff!
O the smoke! the smoke!

Thank heaven the fire is still alight, and burning beautifully bright.
So here we'll lay our burdens down, with eager hearts delighted,
And dip the vine-torch in the pot, and get it there ignited.
Then all together at the gates like battering rams we'll butt.
And if our summons they reject, and keep the barriers shut,
We'll burn the very doors with fire, and them with smoke we'll
smother.
So lay the burdens down. Pheugh! Pheugh! O how this
smoke does bother!
What general from the Samian lines an active hand will lend us?
Well, well, I'm glad my back is freed from all that weight
tremendous.
O pot, 'tis now your turn to help: O send a livelier jet
Of flame this way, that I to-day the earliest light may get.
O Victory, immortal Queen, assist us Thou in rearing
A trophy o'er these woman-hosts, so bold and domineering.

*(During the last few lines the men have been completing their preparations, and the air
above them is now growing lurid with the smoke and the flame of their torches. As the
Men relapse into silence, the voices of Women are heard in the distance. They come
sweeping round from the north side of the Acropolis, carrying their pitchers of water,
and singing, in turn, their entrance song. The two Choruses are for the present
concealed from each other by the north-western angle of the Acropolis.)*

---

like our " fie," " faugh." It is obviously intended to represent the sound of the old
men ΦΥσώντων.

CHORUS OF WOMEN. Redly up in the sky the flames are beginning to flicker,
  Smoke and vapour of fire! come quicker, my friends, come quicker.

      Fly, Nicodice, fly,
      Else will Calyce burn,
      Else Critylla will die,
      Slain by the laws so stern,
      Slain by the old men's hate.
  Ah, but I fear! I fear! can it chance that I come too late?
  Trouble it was, forsooth, before my jug I could fill,
  All in the dusk of the morn, at the spring by the side of the hill,
      What with the clatter of pitchers,
      The noise and press of the throng,
      Jostling with knaves and slaves,
      Till at last I snatched it along,
      Abundance of water supplying
      To friends who are burning and dying.

      Yea, for hither, they state,
      Dotards are dragging, to burn us,
      Logs of enormous weight,
      Fit for a bath-room furnace,
      Vowing to roast and to slay
  Sternly the reprobate women. O Lady, O Goddess, I pray,
  Ne'er may I see them in flames! I hope to behold them with gladness,
  Hellas and Athens redeeming from battle and murder and madness.
      This is the cause why they venture,
      Lady, thy mansions to hold,
      Tritogeneia, Eternal
      Champion with helmet of gold!

And O, if with fire men invade them,
O help us with water to aid them.

(At this juncture the Women wheel round the corner of the Acropolis, and the two Choruses suddenly meet face to face.)

Stop! easy all! what have we here? *(To the Men.)* You vile, abandoned crew,

No good and virtuous men, I'm sure, would act in the way you do.

MEN CH. Hey, here's an unexpected sight! hey, here's a demonstration!
A swarm of women issuing out with warlike preparation!

W. CH. Hallo, you seem a little moved! does this one troop affright you?
You see not yet the myriadth part of those prepared to fight you.

MEN CH. Now, really, Phædrias, shall we stop to hear such odious treason?
Let's break our sticks about their backs, let's beat the jades to reason.

W. CH. Hi, sisters, set the pitchers down, and then they won't embarrass
Our nimble fingers, if the rogues attempt our ranks to harass.

MEN CH. I warrant, now, if twice or thrice we slap their faces neatly,
That they will learn, like Bupalus,' to hold their tongues discreetly.

W. CH. Well, here's my face : I won't draw back : now slap it if you dare,
And I won't leave one ounce of you for other dogs to tear.

MEN CH. Keep still, or else your musty Age to very shreds I'll batter.

W. CH. Now only touch Stratyllis, sir; just lift one finger at her !

MEN CH. And what if with these fists, my love, I pound the wench to shivers ?

W. CH. By Heaven, we'll gnaw your entrails out, and rip away your livers.

---

¹ If we smite them on the cheek, as Hipponax, that *acer hostis Bupalo,* threatened in his lampoons to smite his unhappy antagonist.

MEN CH. There is not than Euripides a bard more wise and knowing,
For women ARE a shameless set, the vilest creatures going.
W. CH. Pick up again, Rhodippe dear, your jug with water brimming.
MEN CH. What made you bring that water here, you God-detested women?
W. CH. What made you bring that light, old Tomb? to set *yourselves* afire?
MEN CH. No, but to kindle for your friends a mighty funeral pyre.
W. CH. Well, then, we brought this water here to put your bonfire out, sirs.
MEN CH. You put our bonfire out, indeed!   W. CH. You'll see, beyond a doubt, sirs.
MEN CH. I swear that with this torch, offhand, I've half a mind to fry you.
W. CH. Got any soap, my lad? if so, a bath I'll soon supply you.
MEN CH. A bath for ME, you mouldy hag!   W. CH. And that a bride-bath, too.
MEN CH. Zounds, did you hear her impudence?   W. CH. Ain't I freeborn as you?
MEN CH. I'll quickly put a stop to this.   W. CH. You'll judge no more, I vow!
MEN CH. Hi! set the vixen's hair on fire.   W. CH. Now, Achelous,[s] now!
MEN CH. Good gracious!   W. CH. What! you find it hot?
MEN CH. Hot? murder! stop! be quiet!
W. CH. I'm watering you, to make you grow.
MEN CH. I wither up from shivering so.
W. CH. I tell you what: a fire you've got,
So warm your members by it.

(At this crisis the tumult is stayed for an instant by the appearance on the stage of a venerable official personage, one of the Magistrates who, after the Sicilian catastrophe,

[s] The name Achelous was used to denote *water* generally. The women are deluging their opponents with cold water from their pitchers.

were appointed, under the name of Probuli, to form a Directory or Committee of Public
Safety. He is attended by four Scythian archers, part of the ordinary police of the
Athenian Republic. The women retire into the background.)

MAGISTRATE. Has then the women's wantonness blazed out,
    Their constant timbrels and Sabaziuses,
    And that Adonis-dirge [9] upon the roof
    Which once I heard in full Assembly-time.
    'Twas when Demostratus (beshrew him) moved
    To sail to Sicily : and from the roof
    A woman, dancing, shrieked *Woe, woe, Adonis !*
    And *he* proposed to enrol Zacynthian hoplites ;
    And *she* upon the roof, the maudlin woman,
    Cried *Wail, Adonis !* yet he forced it through,
    That God-detested, vile Ill-temprian.
    Such are the wanton follies of the sex.

MEN CH. What if you heard their insolence to-day,
    Their vile, outrageous goings on ? And look,
    See how they've drenched and soused us from their pitchers,
    Till we can wring out water from our clothes.

MAG. Ay, by Poseidon, and it serves us right.
    'Tis all our fault : they'll never know their place,
    These pampered women, whilst we spoil them so.
    Hear how we talk in every workman's shop.
    Goldsmith, says one, *this necklace that you made,*
    My gay young wife was dancing yester-eve,
    And lost, sweet soul, the fastening of the clasp ;
    Do please reset it, Goldsmith. Or, again,
    O Shoemaker, my wife's new sandal pinches
    Her little toe, the tender, delicate child,

---

[9] Plutarch, in his Life of Nicias (chap. 13), describes these and similar omens of
ill which preceded the Athenian expedition to Sicily. And he also (chap. 12) tells
us that the orator Demostratus took a leading part in recommending that fatal
measure.

Make it fit easier, please.—Hence all this nonsense !
Yea, things have reached a pretty pass, indeed,
When I, the State's Director, wanting money
To purchase oar-blades, find the Treasury gates
Shut in my face by these preposterous women.
Nay, but no dallying now : bring up the crowbars,
And I'll soon stop *your* insolence, my dears.

(He turns to the Scythians, who, instead of setting to work, are looking idly around them.)

What ! gaping, fool ? and *you*, can *you* do nothing
But stare about with tavern-squinting eye ?
Push in the crowbars underneath the gates,
You, stand that side and heave them : I'll stop here
And heave them here.

(The gates are thrown open, and Lysistrata comes out.)

Lys.   O let your crowbars be.
Lo, I come out unfetched ! What need of crowbars ?
'Tis wits, not crowbars, that ye need to-day.

MAG.   Ay, truly, traitress, say you so ? Here, Archer !
Arrest her, tie her hands behind her back.

LYS.   And if he touch me with his finger-tip,
The public scum ! fore Artemis, he'll rue it.

MAG.   What, man, afeared ? why, catch her round the waist.
And *you* go with him, quick, and bind her fast.

CAL.   *(Coming out.)* And if you do but lay one hand upon her,
Fore Pandrosus, I'll stamp your vitals out.

MAG.   Vitals, ye hag ? Another Archer, ho !
Seize this one first, because she chatters so.

MYRRH.   *(Coming out.)* And if you touch her with your finger-tip,
Fore Phosphorus, you'll need a cupping shortly.

MAG.   Tcha ! what's all this ? lay hold of this one, Archer !
I'll stop this sallying out, depend upon it.

STRATYLLIS. *(Coming out.)* And if he touch her, fore the Queen of Tauris,
I'll pull his squealing hairs out, one by one.

Mag. O dear! all's up! I've never an archer left.
Nay, but I swear we won't be done by women.
Come, Scythians, close your ranks, and all together
Charge! Lys. Charge away, my hearties, and
you'll soon
Know that we've here, impatient for the fight,
Four woman-squadrons, armed from top to toe.

Mag. Attack them, Scythians, twist their hands behind them.

Lys. Forth to the fray, dear sisters, bold allies!
O egg-and-seed-and-potherb-market-girls,
O garlic-selling-barmaid-baking-girls,
Charge to the rescue, smack and whack, and thwack
them,
Slang them, I say: show them what jades ye be.

(The Woman Chorus come forward. After a short struggle the archers are routed.)

Fall back! retire! forbear to strip the slain.

Mag. Hillo! my archers got the worst of that.

Lys. What did the fool expect? Was it to fight
With SLAVES you came? Think you we Women feel
No thirst for glory? Mag. Thirst enough, I trow:
No doubt of that, when there's a tavern handy.

Men Ch. O thou who wastest many words, Director of this nation,
Why wilt thou with such brutes as these thus hold negotiation?
Dost thou not see the bath wherewith the sluts have dared to
lave me,
Whilst all my clothes were on, and ne'er a bit of soap they gave
me?

W. Ch. For 'tis not right, nor yet polite, to strike a harmless neigh-
bour,
And if you do, 'tis needful too that she your eyes belabour.
Full fain would I, a maiden shy, in maiden peace be resting,
Not making here the slightest stir, nor any soul molesting,

D

Unless indeed some rogue should strive to rifle and despoil
   my hive.

*(The field is now open for a suspension of hostilities, and a parley takes place between the
leaders of the two contending factions.)*

MEN CH. O how shall we treat, Lord Zeus, such creatures as these?
   Let us ask the cause for which they have dared to seize,
   To seize this fortress of ancient and high renown,
   This shrine where never a foot profane hath trod,
   The lofty-rocked, inaccessible Cranaan town,
      The holy Temple of God.

   Now to examine them closely and narrowly,
         probing them here and sounding them there,
   Shame if we fail to completely unravel the
         intricate web of this tangled affair.

MAG. Foremost and first I would wish to inquire of them,
         what is this silly disturbance about?
   Why have ye ventured to seize the Acropolis,
         locking the gates and barring us out?

LYS. Keeping the silver securely in custody,
         lest for its sake ye continue the war.

MAG. What, is the war for the sake of the silver, then?
      LYS. Yes; and all other disputes that there are.
   Why is Peisander for ever embroiling us,
         why do the rest of our officers feel
   Always a pleasure in strife and disturbances?
         Simply to gain an occasion to steal.
   Act as they please for the future, the treasury
         never a penny shall yield them, I vow.

MAG. How, may I ask, will you hinder their getting it?
      LYS. We will ourselves be the Treasurers now.

MAG. You, woman, you be the treasurers?   LYS. Certainly.
      Ah, you esteem us unable, perchance!

Are we not skilled in domestic economy,
    do we not manage the household finance ?

MAG. O, that is different.   LYS. Why is it different ?

    MAG. This is required for the fighting, my dear.

LYS. Well, but the fighting itself isn't requisite.

    MAG. Only, without it, we're ruined, I fear.

LYS. WE will deliver you.   MAG. You will deliver us !

    LYS. Truly we will.   MAG. What a capital notion !

LYS. Whether you like it or not, we'll deliver you.

    MAG. Impudent hussy !   LYS. You seem in commotion.

Nevertheless we will do as we promise you.

    MAG. That were a terrible shame, by Demeter.

LYS. Friend, we must save you.   MAG. But how if I wish it not ?

    LYS. That will but make our resolve the completer.

MAG. Fools ! what on earth can possess you to meddle with
    matters of war, and matters of peace ?

LYS. Well, I will tell you the reason.   MAG. And speedily,
    else you will rue it.   LYS. Then listen, and cease

Clutching and clenching your fingers so angrily ;
    keep yourself peaceable.   MAG. Hanged if I can ;

Such is the rage that I feel at your impudence.

    STRAT. Then it is *you* that will rue it, my man.

MAG. Croak your own fate, you ill-omened antiquity.

    (To Lysistrata.) You be the spokeswoman, lady.   LYS. I will.

Think of our old moderation and gentleness,
    think how we bore with your pranks, and were
        still,

All through the days of your former pugnacity,
    all through the war that is over and spent :

Not that (be sure) we approved of your policy ;
    never our griefs you allowed us to vent.

Well we perceived your mistakes and mismanagement.
    Often at home on our housekeeping cares,

Often we heard of some foolish proposal you
    made for conducting the public affairs.
Then would we question you mildly and pleasantly,
    inwardly grieving, but outwardly gay ;
Husband, how goes it abroad ? we would ask of him ;
    what have ye done in Assembly to-day ?
What would ye write on the side of the Treaty stone ?
    Husband says angrily, *What's that to you ?*
You, hold your tongue ! And I held it accordingly.
    STRAT. That is a thing which I NEVER would do !

{ MAG. Ma'am, if you hadn't, you'd soon have repented it.

    LYS. Therefore I held it, and spake not a word.
Soon of another tremendous absurdity,
    wilder and worse than the former we heard.
Husband, I say, with a tender solicitude,
    Why have ye passed such a foolish decree ?
Viciously, moodily, glaring askance at me,
    Stick to your spinning, my mistress, says he,
Else you will speedily find it the worse for you,
    WAR IS THE CARE AND THE BUSINESS OF MEN ! [1]

MAG. Zeus ! 'twas a worthy reply, and an excellent !

    LYS. What ! you unfortunate, shall we not then,
Then, when we see you perplexed and incompetent,
    shall we not tender advice to the State ?
So when aloud in the streets and the thoroughfares
    sadly we heard you bewailing of late,
Is there a Man to defend and deliver us ?
    No, says another, *there's none in the land ;*

---

[1] From the speech of Hector to Andromache, in the Sixth Iliad, thus rendered by Sir J. F. W. Herschel :—

    Resume the cares of thy household :
Look to thy distaff and web, and keep thy maids to their duties,
Each to her task : for Men are the cares of war and its labours.

Then by the Women assembled in conference
jointly a great Revolution was planned,
Hellas to save from her grief and perplexity.
Where is the use of a longer delay?
Shift for the future our parts and our characters;
you, as the women, in silence obey;
We, as the men, will harangue and provide for you;
then shall the State be triumphant again,
Then shall we do what is best for the citizens.

MAG. Women to do what is best for the men!
That were a shameful reproach and unbearable!

LYS. Silence,[2] old gentleman.   MAG. Silence for you?
Stop for a wench with a wimple enfolding her?
No, by the Powers, may I DIE if I do!

LYS. Do not, my pretty one, do not, I pray,
Suffer my wimple to stand in the way.
Here, take it, and wear it, and gracefully tie it,
Enfolding it over your head, and be quiet.
Now to your task.

CAL. Here is an excellent spindle to pull.

MYRR. Here is a basket for carding the wool.

LYS. Now to your task.
Haricots chawing up, petticoats drawing up,
Off to your carding, your combing, your trimming,
WAR IS THE CARE AND THE BUSINESS OF WOMEN.

(During the foregoing lines the women have been arraying the Magistrate in the garb and with the apparatus of a spinning-woman: just as in the corresponding system, below, they bedeck him in the habiliments of a corpse.)

W. CH. Up, up, and leave the pitchers there,
and on, resolved and eager,

---

[2] Lysistrata is putting her system into immediate practice, and therefore addresses the same language and assigns the same duties to the Magistrate, as the Men had been accustomed aforetime to address and assign to the Women.

Our own allotted part to bear
in this illustrious leaguer.

I will dance with resolute, tireless feet all day;
My limbs shall never grow faint, my strength give way;
I will march all lengths with the noble hearts and the true,
For theirs is the ready wit and the patriot hand,
And womanly grace, and courage to dare and do,
And Love of our own bright land.

Children of stiff and intractable grandmothers,
heirs of the stinging viragoes that bore you,
On, with an eager, unyielding tenacity,
wind in your sails, and the haven before you.

LYS. Only let Love, the entrancing, the fanciful,
only let Queen Aphrodite to-day
Breathe on our persons a charm and a tenderness,
lend us their own irresistible sway,
Drawing the men to admire us and long for us;
then shall the war everlastingly cease,
Then shall the people revere us and honour us,
givers of Joy, and givers of Peace.

MAG. Tell us the mode and the means of your doing it.
  LYS. First we will stop the disorderly crew,
Soldiers in arms promenading and marketing.
  STRAT. Yea, by divine Aphrodite, 'tis true.

LYS. Now in the market you see them like Corybants,
jangling about with their armour of mail.
Fiercely they stalk in the midst of the crockery,
sternly parade by the cabbage and kail.

MAG. Right, for a soldier should always be soldierly!
  LYS. Troth, 'tis a mighty ridiculous jest,
Watching them haggle for shrimps in the market-place,
grimly accoutred with shield and with crest.

STRAT. Lately I witnessed a captain of cavalry,
　　　　　proudly the while on his charger he sat,
　　Witnessed him, soldierly, buying an omelet,
　　　　　stowing it all in his cavalry hat.
　　Comes, like a Tereus, a Thracian irregular,
　　　　　shaking his dart and his target to boot;
　　Off runs a shop-girl, appalled at the sight of him,
　　　　　down he sits soldierly, gobbles her fruit.
MAG. You, I presume, could adroitly and gingerly
　　　　　settle this intricate, tangled concern:
　　You in a trice could relieve our perplexities.
　　　　　Lys. Certainly. MAG. How? permit me to learn.
LYS. Just as a woman, with nimble dexterity,
　　　　　thus with her hands disentangles a skein,
　　Hither and thither her spindles unravel it,
　　　　　drawing it out, and pulling it plain.
　　So would this weary Hellenic entanglement
　　　　　soon be resolved by our womanly care,
　　So would our embassies neatly unravel it,
　　　　　drawing it here and pulling it there.
MAG. Wonderful, marvellous feats, not a doubt of it,
　　　　　you with your skeins and your spindles can show;
　　Fools! do you really expect to unravel a
　　　　　terrible war like a bundle of tow?
LYS. Ah, if you only could manage your politics
　　　　　just in the way that we deal with a fleece!
MAG. Tell us the recipe. LYS. First, in the washing-tub
　　　　　plunge it, and scour it, and cleanse it from
　　　　　grease,
　　Purging away all the filth and the nastiness;
　　　　　then on the table expand it and lay,
　　Beating out all that is worthless and mischievous,
　　　　　picking the burrs and the thistles away.

Next, for the clubs, the cabals, and the coteries,
    banding unrighteously, office to win,
Treat them as clots in the wool, and dissever them,
    lopping the heads that are forming therein.
Then you should card it, and comb it, and mingle it,
    all in one Basket of love and of unity,
Citizens, visitors, strangers, and sojourners,
    all the entire, undivided community.
Know you a fellow in debt to the Treasury?
    Mingle him merrily in with the rest.
Also remember the cities, our colonies,
    outlying states in the east and the west,
Scattered about to a distance surrounding us,
    these are our shreds and our fragments of
    wool;
These to one mighty political aggregate
    tenderly, carefully, gather and pull,
Twining them all in one thread of good fellowship;
    thence a magnificent bobbin to spin,
Weaving a garment of comfort and dignity,
    worthily wrapping the People therein.

MAG. Heard any ever the like of their impudence,
    these who have nothing to do with the war,
Preaching of bobbins, and beatings, and washing-tubs?
    LYS. Nothing to do with it, wretch that you are!
We are the people who feel it the keenliest,
    doubly on us the affliction is cast;
Where are the sons that we sent to your battle-fields?
    MAG. Silence! a truce to the ills that are past.

LYS. Then in the glory and grace of our womanhood,
    all in the May and the morning of life,
Lo, we are sitting forlorn and disconsolate,
    what has a soldier to do with a wife?

We might endure it, but ah! for the younger ones,
  still in their maiden apartments they stay,
Waiting the husband that never approaches them,
  watching the years that are gliding away.

MAG. Men, I suppose, have their youth everlastingly.

LYS. Nay, but it isn't the same with a man :
Gray though he be when he comes from the battle-field,
  still if he wishes to marry, he can.
Brief is the spring and the flower of our womanhood,
  once let it slip, and it comes not again ;
Sit as we may with our spells and our auguries,
  never a husband will marry us then.

MAG. Truly whoever is able to wed—[3]

LYS. Truly, old fellow, 'tis time you were dead.
So a pig shall be sought, and an urn shall be bought,
And I'll bake you and make you a funeral cake.
      Take it and go.

CAL. Here are the fillets all ready to wear.

MYRR. Here is the chaplet to bind in your hair.

  LYS. Take it and go.
What are you prating for ?   What are you waiting
  for ?
Charon is staying, delaying his crew,
Charon is calling and bawling for you.

MAG. See, here's an outrage ! here's a scandalous shame !
I'll run and show my fellow magistrates
The woeful, horrid, dismal plight I'm in.

LYS. Grumbling because we have not laid you out ?
Wait for three days, and then with dawn will come,
All in good time, the third-day funeral rites.

---

[3] Apparently he was about to add, "will soon find a wife," but Lysistrata interrupts him, and she and her companions dress him up like a corpse.

(The Magistrate runs off in his grave-clothes to complain of and exhibit the treatment he has received. Lysistrata and her friends withdraw into the Acropolis. The two Choruses remain without, and relieve the tedium of the siege with a little banter.)

MEN CH. This is not a time for slumber;
                now let all the bold and free,
Strip to meet the great occasion,
                vindicate our rights with me.
I can smell a deep, surprising
Tide of Revolution rising,
Odour as of folk devising
                Hippias's tyranny.
And I feel a dire misgiving,
Lest some false Laconians, meeting
                in the house of Cleisthenes,
Have inspired these wretched women
                all our wealth and pay to seize,
Pay from whence I get my living.
Gods! to hear these shallow wenches
                taking citizens to task,
Prattling of a brassy buckler,
                jabbering of a martial casque!
Gods! to think that they have ventured
                with Laconian men to deal,
Men of just the faith and honour
                that a ravening wolf might feel!
Plots they're hatching, plots contriving,
                plots of rampant Tyranny;
But o'er us they shan't be Tyrants,
                no, for on my guard I'll be,
And I'll dress my sword in myrtle,
                and with firm and dauntless hand,
Here beside Aristogeiton
                resolutely take my stand,

Marketing in arms beside him.
This the time and this the place
When my patriot arm must deal a
—blow [4] upon that woman's face.

W. Ch. Ah, your mother shall not know you,
impudent! when home you go.
Strip, my sisters, strip for action,
on the ground your garments throw.
Right it is that I my slender
Tribute to the state should render,
I, who to her thoughtful tender
care my happiest memories owe;
Bore, at seven, the mystic casket;
Was, at ten, our Lady's miller;
then the yellow Brauron bear;
Next (a maiden tall and stately
with a string of figs to wear)
Bore in pomp the holy Basket.
Well may such a gracious City
all my filial duty claim.
What though I was born a woman,
comrades, count it not for blame
If I bring the wiser counsels;
I an equal share confer
Towards the common stock of Athens,
I contribute men to her.
But the noble contribution,
but the olden tribute-pay,
Which your fathers' fathers left you,
relic of the Median fray,

[4] Unexpectedly suits the action to the word. A similar result takes place at the end of the three succeeding speeches.

Dotards, ye have lost and wasted !
    nothing in its stead ye bring,
Nay ourselves ye're like to ruin,
    spend and waste by blundering.
Murmuring are ye ?   Let me hear you,
    only let me hear you speak,
And from this unpolished slipper
    comes a—slap upon your cheek !

MEN CH.   Is not this an outrage sore ?
    And methinks it blows not o'er,
    But increases more and more.
Come, my comrades, hale and hearty,
    on the ground your mantles throw,
In the odour of their manhood
    men to meet the fight should go,
Not in these ungodly wrappers
    swaddled up from top to toe.

On, then on, my white-foot veterans,[5] ye who thronged Leipsydrium's
    height
In the days when we were Men !
Shake this chill old Age from off you,
Spread the wings of youth again.

O these women ! give them once a
    handle howsoever small,
And they'll soon be nought behind us
    in the manliest feats of all.
Yea, they'll build them fleets and navies
    and they'll come across the sea,

---

[5] λευκόποδες, with a play on λυκόποδες, the name given to the outlawed Alc-
mæonids when they returned to Attica and established themselves on Leipsydrium,
in their first fruitless attempt to overthrow the tyranny of Hippias.

Come like Carian Artemisia,
> fighting in their ships with me.
Or they'll turn their first attention,
> haply, to equestrian fights,
If they do, I know the issue,
> there's an end of all the knights!
Well a woman sticks on horseback :
> look around you, see, behold,
Where on Micon's living friezes
> fight the Amazons of old !
Shall we let these wilful women,
> O, my brothers, do the same ?
Rather first their necks we'll rivet
> tightly in the pillory frame.

W. Ch.   If our smouldering fires ye wake,
> Soon our wildbeast wrath will break
> Out against you, and we'll make,
Make you howl to all your neighbours,
> currycombed, poor soul, and tanned.
Throw aside your mantles, sisters,
> come, a firm determined band,
In the odour of your wrathful
> snappish womanhood to stand.

Who'll come forth and fight me ? garlic, nevermore, nor beans for him.
> Nay, if one sour word ye say,
I'll be like the midwife beetle,
> Following till the eagle lay.

Yea, for you and yours I reck not
> whilst my Lampito survives,
And my noble, dear Ismenia,
> loveliest of the Theban wives.

Keep decreeing seven times over,
    not a bit of good you'll do,
Wretch abhorred of all the people
    and of all our neighbours too.
So that when in Hecate's honour
    yesterday I sent to get
From our neighbours in Bœotia
    such a dainty darling pet,
Just a lovely, graceful, slender,
    whitefleshed eel divinely tender,
Thanks to your decrees, confound them,
    one and all refused to send her.
And you'll never stop from making
    these absurd decrees I know,
Till I catch your leg and toss you
    —Zeus-ha'-mercy, there you go !

(An interval of several days must here be supposed to elapse. The separation of the sexes has now become insupportable to both parties, and the only question is which side will hold out the longest. The Chorus of Women are alarmed at seeing Lysistrata come on the stage, and walk up and down with an anxious and troubled air. The first twelve lines of the dialogue which ensues are borrowed and burlesqued from Euripides.)

W. Ch.   Illustrious leader of this bold emprize
        What brings thee forth, with trouble in thine eyes ?
Lys.   Vile women's works : tho feminine hearts they show :
        These make me pace, dejected, to and fro.
W. Ch.   O what ! and O what !
Lys.   'Tis true ! 'tis true !
W. Ch.   O to your friends, great queen, the tale unfold.
Lys.   'Tis sad to tell, and sore to leave untold.
W. Ch.   What, what has happened ? tell us, tell us quick.
Lys.   Ay, in one word. The girls are—husband-sick.
W. Ch.   O Zeus ! Zeus ! O !
Lys.   Why call on Zeus ? the fact is surely so.

I can no longer keep the minxes in.
They slip out everywhere.   One I discovered
Down by Pan's grotto, burrowing through the loophole :
Another, wriggling down by crane and pulley :
A third deserts outright : a fourth I dragged
Back by the hair, yestreen, just as she started
On sparrow's back, straight for Orsilochus's :
They make all sorts of shifts to get away.

(A woman is seen attempting to cross the stage.)

Ha! here comes one, deserting.   Hi there, Hi !
Where are you off to ?   FIRST WOMAN *(hurriedly)*. I must just
    run home.
I left some fine Milesian wools about,
I'm sure the moths are at them.   LYS. Moths indeed !
Get back.   FIRST W. But really I'll return directly,
I only want to spread them on the couch.

LYS.   No spreadings out, no runnings home to-day.

FIRST W. What ! leave my wools to perish ?   LYS. If needs be.

(A second woman now attempts to cross the stage.)

SECONDW. O goodness gracious ! O that lovely flax
    I left at home unhackled !   LYS. Here's another!
She's stealing off to hackle flax forsooth.

(To the second woman.)

Come, come, get back.   SECOND W. O yes, and so I will,
I'll comb it out and come again directly.

LYS.   Nay, nay, no combing : once begin with that
    And other girls are sure to want the same.

(Several women enter one after the other.)

THIRDW. O holy Eileithyia, stay my labour
    Till I can reach some lawful travail-place.

LYS.   How now !   THIRD W. My pains are come.   LYS. Why
        yesterday
    You were not pregnant.   THIRD W. But to-day I am.

Quick, let me pass, Lysistrata, at once
To find a midwife.   LYS. What's it all about?
What's this hard lump?   THIRD W. That's a male child.
  LYS. Not it.
It's something made of brass, and hollow too.
Come, come, out with it. O you silly woman,
What! cuddling up the sacred helmet there
And say you're pregnant?   THIRD W. Well, and so I am.

LYS.   What's this for then?   THIRD W. Why, if my pains
          o'ertake me
In the Acropolis, I'd creep inside
And sit and hatch there as the pigeons do.

LYS.   Nonsense and stuff : the thing's as plain as can be.
Stay and keep here the name-day of your—helmet.

FOURTH W. But I can't sleep a single wink up here,
So scared I was to see the holy serpent.

FIFTH W. And I shall die for lack of rest, I know,
With this perpetual hooting of the owls.

LYS.   O ladies, ladies, cease these tricks, I pray.
Ye want your husbands. And do you suppose
They don't want *us*? · Full wearisome, I know,
Their nights without us. O bear up, dear friends,
Be firm, be patient, yet one little while,
For I've an oracle (here 'tis) which says
We're sure to conquer if we hold together.

WOMEN. O read us what it says.   LYS. Then all keep silence.

(*Lysistrata reads out the oracle.*)

Soon as the swallows are seen collecting and crouching together,
Shunning the hoopoes' flight and keeping aloof from the Love-birds,
Cometh a rest from ill, and Zeus the Lord of the Thunder
Changeth the upper to under.   WOMEN. Preserve us, shall *we* be the
     upper?

LYS. *Nay, but if once they wrangle, and flutter away in dissension*

Out of the Temple of God, then all shall see and acknowledge,
Never a bird of the air so perjured and frail as the swallow.
WOMEN. Wow, but that's plain enough ! O all ye Gods,
     Let us not falter in our efforts now.
     Come along in. O friends, O dearest friends,
     'Twere sin and shame to fail the oracle.

(The women, with Lysistrata, re-enter the Acropolis. The two Choruses again indulge
in an interchange of banter. The Men begin.)

MEN CH. Now to tell a little story
     Fain, fain I grow,
    One I heard when quite an urchin
     Long, long ago.
     How that once
    All to shun the nuptial bed
    From his home Melanion fled,
    To the hills and deserts sped,
     Kept his dog,
     Wove his snares,
     Set his nets,
     Trapped his hares ;
    Home he nevermore would go,
    He detested women so.
    We are of Melanion's mind,
     We detest the womankind.
MAN. May I, mother, kiss your cheek ?
WOMAN. Then you won't require a leek.[6]
MAN. Hoist my leg, and kick you, so ?
WOMAN. Fie ! what stalwart legs you show !
MAN. Just such stalwart legs and strong,
     Just such stalwart legs as these,

[6] To produce artificial tears : you shall shed real ones. So, in the converse case
of a fictitious grief Shakespeare says, "The tears live in an onion that should water
this sorrow."—A. and C., i. 2.

F

To the noble chiefs belong,
Phormio and Myronides.

(It is now the women's turn. The two systems are of course antistrophical.

W. Ch. Now to tell a little story
Fain, fain am I,
To your tale about Melanion
Take this reply.
How that once
Savage Timon, all forlorn,
Dwelt amongst the prickly thorn
Visage-shrouded, Fury-born.
Dwelt alone,
Far away,
Cursing men
Day by day;
Never saw his home again,
Kept aloof from haunts of men :
Hating men of evil mind,
Dear to all the womankind.
Woman. Shall I give your cheek a blow?
Man. No, I thank you, no, no, no!
Woman. Hoist my foot and kick you too?
Man. Fie! what vulgar feet I view.
Woman. Vulgar feet! absurd, absurd,
Don't such foolish things repeat;
Never were, upon my word,
Tinier, tidier little feet.

*(The two Choruses now retire into the background : and there is again a short pause.
Suddenly the voice of Lysistrata is heard calling eagerly to her friends.)*

Lys. Ho, ladies! ladies! quick, this way, this way!
Woman. O what's the matter and what means that cry?
Lys. A man! a man! I see a man approaching

Wild with desire, beside himself with love.
O lady of Cyprus, Paphos, and Cythera,
Keep on, straight on, the way you are going now!

WOMAN. But where's the man? LYS. (*pointing*.) Down there, by
    Chloe's chapel.

WOMAN. O so he is : who ever can he be !

LYS. Know you him, any one? MYRR. O yes, my dear,
    I know him. That's Cinesias, my husband.

LYS. O then 'tis yours to roast and bother him well ;
    Coaxing, yet coy : enticing, fooling him,
    Going all lengths, save what our Oath forbids.

MYRR. Ay, ay, trust *me*. LYS. And I'll assist you, dear ;
    I'll take my station here, and help befool
    And roast our victim. All the rest, retire.

(*The others withdraw, leaving Lysistrata alone upon the wall. Cinesias approaches
underneath.*)

CINESIAS. O me ! these pangs and paroxysms of love,
    Riving my heart, keen as a torturer's wheel !

LYS. Who's this within the line of sentries ? CIN. I.

LYS. A man ? CIN. A man, no doubt. LYS. Then get you gone.

CIN. Who bids me go ? LYS. I, guard on outpost duty.

CIN. O call me out, I pray you, Myrrhina.

LYS. Call you out Myrrhina ! And who are you ?

CIN. Why I'm her husband, I'm Cinesias.

LYS. O welcome, welcome, dearest man ; your name
    Is not unknown nor yet unhonoured here.
    Your wife for ever has it on her lips.
    She eats no egg, no apple, but she says
    This to Cinesias ! CIN. O, good heaven ! good heaven !

LYS. She does, indeed : and if we ever chance
    To talk of men, she vows that all the rest
    Are veriest trash beside Cinesias.

CIN. Ah ! call her out. LYS. And will you give me aught ?

CIN. O yes, I'll give you anything I've got.

LYS. Then I'll go down and call her.   CIN. Pray be quick
I have no joy, no happiness in life,
Since she, my darling, left me. When I enter
My vacant home, I weep ; and all the world
Seems desolate and bare : my very meals
Give me no joy, now Myrrhina is gone.

MYRR. (*Within.*) Ay, ay, I love, I love him, but he won't
Be loved by me : call me not out to him.

CIN. What mean you, Myrrhina, my sweet, sweet love ?
Do, do come down.   MYRR. No, no, sir, not to you.

CIN. What, won't you when I call you, Myrrhina ?

MYRR. Why, though you call me, yet you want me not.

CIN. Not want you, Myrrhina ! I'm dying for you.

MYRR. Goodbye.   CIN. Nay, nay, but listen to the child
At all events : speak to Mama, my child.

CHILD. Mama ! Mama ! Mama !

CIN. Have you no feeling, mother, for your child,
Six days unwashed, unsuckled ?   MYRR. Ay, 'tis I
That feel for baby, 'tis Papa neglects him.

CIN. Come down and take him, then ?   MYRR. O what it is
To be a mother ! I must needs go down.

(*She descends from the wall, and four lines below reappears through the gate. While she is
gone, Cinesias speaks.*)

CIN. She looks, methinks, more youthful than she did,
More gentle-loving, and more sweet by far.
Her very airs, her petulant, saucy ways,
They do but make me love her, love her more.

MYRR. O my sweet child, a naughty father's child,
Mama's own darling, let me kiss you, pet.

CIN. Why treat me thus, you baggage, letting others
Lead you astray : making me miserable
And yourself too ?   MYRR. Hands off ! don't touch me, sir.

Cin.	And all our household treasures, yours and mine,
	Are gone to wrack and ruin. Myrr. I don't care.
Cin.	Not care, although the fowls are in the house
	Pulling your threads to pieces? Myrr. Not a bit.
Cin.	Nor though the sacred rites of wedded love
	Have been so long neglected? won't you come?
Myrr.	No, no, I won't, unless you stop the war,
	And all make friends. Cin. Well, then, if such your will,
	We'll e'en do this. Myrr. Well, then, if such your will,
	I'll e'en come home : but now I've sworn I won't.
Cin.	Yet kiss me, Myrrhina, unkissed so long.
Myrr.	There (*kisses him*). Cin. O my darling, come, come home at once.

(*After trifling with him a little longer, Myrrhina suddenly disappears into the Acropolis, leaving him in a mood to vote for peace with Sparta on any terms, so that he may get her home again. A Laconian herald is next seen approaching, and the Magistrate comes forward to meet him.*)

Herald.	Whaur sall a body fin' the Athanian senate,
	Or the gran' lairds? Ha' gotten news to tell.
Mag.	News, have you, friend? And what in the world are you ?
Her.	A heralt, billie ! jist a Spartian heralt,
	Come, by the Twa', anent a Peace, ye ken.
Mag.	Ay, and how fare the Spartans ? tell me that :
	And tell me truly, for I know the fact.
Her.	They're bad eneugh, they canna weel be waur ;
	They're sair bestead, Spartians, allies, an' a'.
Mag.	And how and whence arose this trouble first ?
	From Pan ? Her. Na, na, 'twer' Lampito, I ween,
	First set it gangin' : then our hizzies, a'
	Risin' like rinners at ane signal word,
	Loupit, an' jibbed, an' dang the men awa'.
Mag.	How like ye that ? Her. Och, we're in waefu' case.
	They stan' abeigh, the lassies do, an' vow
	They'll no be couthie wi' the laddies mair

Till a' mak' Peace, and throughly en' the War.

MAG.   This is a plot they have everywhere been hatching,
These villanous women : now I see it all.
Run home, my man, and bid your people send
Envoys with absolute powers to treat for peace,
And I will off with all the speed I can,
And get our Council here to do the same.

HER.   Nebbut, I'se fly, ye rede me weel, I'm thinkin'.

(The Herald leaves for Sparta; the Magistrate returns to the Senate; and the two Choruses now advance for a final skirmish.)

MEN CH. There is nothing so resistless as a woman in her ire,
She is wilder than a leopard, she is fiercer than a fire.

W. CH. And yet you're so daft as with women to contend,
When 'tis in your power to win me and have me as a friend.

MEN CH. I'll never, never cease all women to detest.

W. CH. That's as you please hereafter : meanwhile you're all undressed.
I really can't allow it, you are getting quite a joke ;
Permit me to approach you and to put you on this cloak.

MEN CH. Now that's not so bad or unfriendly I declare ;
It was only from bad temper that I stripped myself so bare.

W. CH. There, now you look a man : and none will joke and jeer you :
And if you weren't so spiteful that no one can come near you,
I'd have pulled out the insect that is sticking in your eye.

MEN CH. Ay, that is what's consuming me, that little biter-fly.
Yes, scoop it out and show me, when you've got him safe away :
The plaguy little brute, he's been biting me all day.

W. CH. I'll do it, sir, I'll do it : but you're a cross one, you.
O Zeus! here's a monster I am pulling forth to view.
Just look ! don't you think 'tis a Tricorysian gnat ?

MEN CH. And he's been dig, dig, digging (so I thank you much for that)
Till the water, now he's gone, keeps running from my eye.

W. CH. But although you've been so naughty, I'll come and wipe it dry,

And I'll kiss you. MEN CH. No, not kiss me! W. CH.
Will you, nill you, it must be.

MEN CH. Get along, a murrain on you. Tcha! what coaxing rogues
are ye!

That was quite a true opinion which a wise man gave about
you,

We can't live with such tormentors, no, by Zeus, nor yet
without you.

Now we'll make a faithful treaty, and for evermore agree,

I will do no harm to women, they shall do no harm to me.

Join our forces, come along : one and all commence the song.

JOINT CHORUS. Not to objurgate and scold you,
Not unpleasant truths to say,
But with words and deeds of bounty
Come we here to-day.
Ah, enough of idle quarrels,
　　Now attend, I pray.
Now whoever wants some money,
Minas two or minas three,
Let them say so, man and woman,
Let them come with me.
Many purses, large and—empty,[7]
In my house they'll see.
Only you must strictly promise,
Only you indeed must say
That whenever Peace re-greet us,
You will—not repay.

[7] Read

πόλλ' ἔσωθεν
KEN' ἔχομεν βαλάντια.

These little twin songs, and the similar pair which will be found a few pages
further on, are all fashioned in the same vein of pleasantry; consisting of large and
liberal offers made by the Chorus, but with an intimation at the end that they have
no means or intention of performing them.　　Χ

Some Carystian friends are coming,
Pleasant gentlemen, to dine;
And I've made some soup, and slaughtered
Such a lovely swine;
Luscious meat ye'll have and tender
At this feast of mine.
Come along, yourselves and children,
Come to grace my board to-day;
Take an early bath, and deck you
In your best array;
Then walk in and ask no questions,
Take the readiest way.
Come along, like men of mettle;
Come as though 'twere all for you:
Come, you'll find my only entrance
Locked and bolted too.

(The Laconian ambassadors are seen approaching.)

Chor. Lo here from Sparta the envoys come: in a pitiful plight they
are hobbling in.
Heavily hangs each reverend beard; heavily droops and trails from
the chin.
Laconian envoys! first I bid you welcome,
And next I ask how goes the world with *you?*
Laconian. I needna mony words to answer that!
'Tis unco plain hoo the warld gangs wi' us.
Chor. Dear, dear, this trouble grows from bad to worse.
Lac. 'Tis awfu' bad: 'tis nae gude talkin', cummer.
We maun hae peace whatever gaet we gang till't.
Chor. And here, good faith, I see our own Autochthons
Bustling along. They seem in trouble too.
(The Athenian ambassadors enter.)
Athenian. Can some good soul inform me where to find

Lysistrata ? our men are (*shrugging his shoulders*) as you see.

(*He perceives the Laconian ambassadors.*)

Aha, Laconians ! a bad business this.

LAC. 'Deed is it, lovey ; though it grow nae waur.

ATH. Well, well, Laconians, come to facts at once.

What brings you here ? LAC. We're envoys sent to claver

Anent a Peace. ATH. Ah, just the same as we.

Then let's call out Lysistrata at once,

There's none but she can make us friends again.

LAC. Ay, by the Twa', ca' oot Lysistrata.

CHOR. Nay, here she is ! no need, it seems, to call.

She heard your voices, and she comes uncalled.

(*Lysistrata comes forward attended by her handmaid Reconciliation.*)

O Lady, noblest and best of all ! arise, arise, and thyself reveal,

Gentle, severe, attractive, harsh, well skilled with all our complaints to deal,

The first and foremost of Hellas come, they are caught by the charm of thy spell-drawn wheel,

They come to Thee to adjust their claims, disputes to settle, and strifes to heal.

LYS. And no such mighty matter, if you take them

In Love's first passion, still unsatisfied.

I'll try them now. Go, RECONCILIATION,

Bring those Laconians hither, not with rude

Ungenial harshness hurrying them along,

Not in the awkward style our husbands used,

But with all tact, as only women can.

So ; so : now bring me those Athenians too.

Now then, Laconians, stand beside me here,

And you stand there, and listen to my words.

I am a woman, but I don't lack sense ;

I'm of myself not badly off for brains,

And often listening to my father's words
And old men's talk, I've not been badly schooled.
And now, dear friends, I wish to chide you both,
That ye, all of one blood, all brethren sprinkling
The selfsame altars from the selfsame laver,
At Pylæ, Pytho, and Olympia, ay
And many others which 'twere long to name,
That ye, Hellenes—with barbarian foes
Armed, looking on—fight and destroy Hellenes!
So far one reprimand includes you both.

ATH. And I, I'm dying all for love, sweetheart.
LYS. And ye, Laconians, for I'll turn to you,
    Do ye not mind how Pericleidas[8] came,
    (His coat was scarlet but his cheeks were white),
    And sat a suppliant at Athenian altars
    And begged for help?   'Twas when Messene pressed
    Weighing you down, and God's great earthquake too.
    And Cimon went, Athenian Cimon went
    With his four thousand men, and saved your State.
    And ye, whom Athens aided, now in turn
    Ravage the land which erst befriended you.
ATH. Fore Zeus they're wrong, they're wrong, Lysistrata.
LAC. O ay, we're wrang, but she's a braw ane, she.
LYS. And you, Athenians, think ye that I mean
    To let You off?   Do ye not mind, when ye
    Wore skirts of hide, how these Laconians[9] came
    And stood beside you in the fight alone,
    And slew full many a stout Thessalian trooper,
    Full many of Hippias's friends and helpers,
    And freed the State, and gave your people back
    The civic mantle for the servile skirt?

[8] See Plutarch, Cimon, chap. 16. Thuc. i. 102; iii. 54.
[9] See Hdt. v. 64, 65.

Lac. Danged, an' there ever waur a bonnier lassie!

Ath. Hanged if I ever saw so sweet a creature!

Lys. Such friends aforetime, helping each the other,
What is it makes you fight and bicker now?
Why can't ye come to terms? Why can't ye, hey?

Lac. Troth an' we're willin', gin they gie us back
Yon girdled neuk.   Ath. What's that?   Lac. Pylus, yo
ninny,
Whilk we've been aye langin' an' graipin' for.

Ath. No, by Poseidon, but you won't get that.

Lys. O let them have it, man.   Ath. How can we stir
Without it?   Lys. Ask for something else instead.

Ath. Hum! haw! let's see; suppose they give us back
Echinus first, then the full-bosomed gulf
Of Melis, then the straight Megaric limbs.

Lac. Eh, mon, ye're daft; ye'll no hae everything.

Lys. O let it be: don't wrangle about the limbs.

Ath. I'fecks, I'd like to strip, and plough my field.

Lac. An' I to bring the midden, by the Twa'.

Lys. All this ye'll do, when once ye come to terms.
So if ye would, go and consult together
And talk it over, each with your allies.

Ath. Allies, says she! Now my good soul consider:
What *do* they want, what *can* they want, but this,
Their wives again?   Lac. The fient anither wiss
Ha' mine, I ween.   Ath. Nor my Carystians either.

Lys. O that is well: so purify yourselves;
And in the Acropolis we'll feast you all
On what our cupboards still retain in store.
There, each to other, plight your oath and troth,
Then every man receive his wife again,
And hie off homeward.   Ath. That we will, and quickly.

Lac. Gae on: we'se follow.   Ath. Ay, as quick as quick.

(Lysistrata and the ambassadors go in.)

CHOR. Gorgeous robes and golden trinkets,
    Shawls and mantles rich and rare,
I will lend to all who need them,
    Lend for youths to wear,
Or if any comrade's daughter
    Would the Basket bear.
One and all I here invite you,
    Freely of my goods partake,
Nought is sealed so well, but boldly
    Ye the seals may break,
And of all that lurks behind them,
    Quick partition make.
Only, if you find the treasures,
Only, if the stores you spy,
You must have, I tell you plainly,
    Keener sight than I.

Is THERE any man among you,
    With a lot of children small,
With a crowd of hungry servants,
    Starving in his hall ?
I have wheat to spare in plenty,
    I will feed them all.
Loaves, a quart apiece, I'll give them,
Come along, whoever will,
Bring your bags, and bring your wallets
    For my slave to fill;
Manes, he's the boy to pack them
    Tight and tighter still.
Only you must keep your distance,
Only you must needs take care,
Only—don't approach my doorway,
    Ware the watch-dog, ware !

(Some idlers come in from the market-place, and attempt to enter the house in which the ambassadors are feasting.)

IDLER. Open the door there, ho ! PORTER. Be off, you rascal !

IDLER. What, won't you stir ? I've half a mind to roast you
All with this torch. No, that's a vulgar trick.
I won't do that. Still if the audience wish it,
To please their tastes we'll undertake the task.

SECOND IDLER. And we, with you, will undertake the task.

PORTER. Hang you, be off ! what are you at ? you'll catch it.
Come, come, begone ; that these Laconians here,
The banquet ended, may depart in peace.

(The banqueters begin to come out.)

FIRST ATH. Well, if I ever saw a feast like this !
What cheery fellows those Laconians were,
And we were wondrous witty in our cups.

SECOND ATH. Ay, ay, 'tis when we're sober, we're so daft.
Now if the State would take a friend's advice,
'Twould make its envoys always all get drunk.
When we go dry to Sparta, all our aim
Is just to see what mischief we can do.
We don't hear aught they say ; and we infer
A heap of things they never said at all.
Then we bring home all sorts of differing tales.
Now everything gives pleasure : if a man,
When he should sing Cleitagora, strike up
With Telamon's song, we'd clap him on the back,
And say 'twas excellent ; ay, and swear it too.

(The idlers again approach.)

PORTER. Why, bless the fellows, here they come again,
Crowding along. Be off, you scoundrels, will you ?

IDLER. By Zeus, we must : the guests are coming out.

(The Ambassadors come out from the banquet.)

LAC. O lovey mine, tak' up the pipes an' blaw.
An' I'se jist dance an' sing a canty sang

Anent the Athanians an' our ainsells too.

ATH. Ay, by the Powers, take up the pipes and blow.
Eh, but I dearly love to see you dance.

LAC.[1] Stir, Memory, stir the chiels
Wi' that auld sang o' thine,
Whilk kens what we an' Attics did
In the gran' fechts lang syne.

At Artemisium They
A' resolute an' strang
Rushed daurly to the fray,
Hurtlin' like Gudes amang
The timmered ships, an' put the Medes to rout.
An' Us Leonidas led out
Like gruesome boars, I ween,
Whettin' our tuskies keen.
Muckle around the chaps was the white freath gleamin',
Muckle adoon the legs was the white freath streamin',
For a' unnumbered as the sands
Were they, thae Persian bands.

O Artemis, the pure, the chaste,
The virgin Queller o' the beasties,
O come wi' power an' come wi' haste,
An' come to join our friendly feasties.
Come wi' thy stoutest tether,
To knit our sauls thegither,
An' gie us Peace in store,
An' Luve for evermore.
Far hence, far hence depart
The tod's deceitfu' heart!

[1] The songs with which the Play concludes are, in the original, representatives
of two widely differing styles of minstrelsy: the light and airy measures of the
Ionians, and the "Dorian movement, bold or grave."

O virgin huntress, pure an' chaste,
O come wi' power, an' come wi' haste.

Lys. There, all is settled, all arranged at last.
Now, take your ladies; you, Laconians, those,
And you, take these; then standing side by side,
Each by his partner, lead your dances out
In grateful honour to the Gods, and O
Be sure you nevermore offend again.

Ath. Now for the Chorus, the Graces, the minstrelsy,
Call upon Artemis, queen of the glade;
Call on her brother, the Lord of festivity,
Holy and gentle one, mighty to aid.
Call upon Bacchus, afire with his Mænades;
Call upon Zeus, in the lightning arrayed;
Call on his queen, ever blessed, adorable;
Call on the holy, infallible Witnesses,
Call them to witness the peace and the harmony,
This which divine Aphrodite has made.
Allala! Lallala! Lallala, Lallala!
Whoop for victory, Lallalalæ!
Evoi! Evoi! Lallala, Lallala!
Evæ! Evæ! Lallalalæ.

Our excellent new song is done;
Do you, Laconian, give us one.

Lac. Leave Taygety, an' quickly
Hither, Muse Laconian, come.
Hymn the Gude o' braw Amyclæ,
Hymn Athana, Brassin-dome.
Hymn the Tyndarids, for ever
Sportin' by Eurotas river.

THE LYSISTRATA.

Noo then, noo the step begin,
Twirlin' licht the fleecy skin;
Sae we'se join our blithesome voices,
Praisin' Sparta, loud an' lang,
Sparta wha of auld rejoices
In the Choral dance an' sang.
O to watch her bonnie dochters
Sport alang Eurotas' waters!
Winsome feet for ever plyin',
Fleet as fillies, wild an' gay,
Winsome tresses tossin', flyin',
As o' Bacchanals at play.
Leda's dochter, on before us,
Pure an' sprety, guides the Chorus.

    Onward go,
Whilst your eager hand represses
A' the glory o' your tresses;
Whilst your eager foot is springin'
    Like the roe;
Whilst your eager voice is singin'
Praise to Her in might excellin'
Goddess o' the Brassin Dwellin'.

GILBERT AND RIVINGTON, PRINTERS, ST. JOHN'S SQUARE, LONDON.

THE CLOUDS OF ARISTOPHANES.

The Greek Text, with a Translation into Corresponding Metres, and Original Notes. Small 4to.

"Not a mere drily correct version, but a spirited piece, which will give the English reader a very good idea of the celebrated 'Clouds,' and, what is of more importance, may be perused with pleasure."—*Spectator.*

"A most successful performance. Not only the meaning and metres of Aristophanes are faithfully represented, but also his tone and spirit: his sparkling wit, his pointed raillery, his broad farce, his poetical flights, and the manly vigour of his sober moods. Even the puns, and other almost untranslateable forms of expression, are not lost to the English reader. Excellent notes are appended to the Greek text."—*Athenæum.*

"A good edition and translation of the 'Clouds.'"—*Dr. Donaldson (Classical Scholarship and Classical Learning).*

ALSO,

THE PEACE OF ARISTOPHANES.

ACTED AT ATHENS AT THE GREAT DIONYSIA, B.C. 421.

The Greek Text Revised, with a Translation into Corresponding Metres, and Original Notes. Small 4to.

"An able, pleasant, and valuable book. It has a well-written Preface; a carefully prepared text; a readable, sometimes striking, translation; and notes which are lively and full of literature. We shall be glad to meet Mr. Rogers on this old classical field again."— *Pall Mall Gazette.*

'The version is so terse as to run almost line for line with the Greek, while it is lively enough to tempt the mere English reader, and accurate enough to give pleasure to the scholar who has the Greek before him. The notes are marked with a pleasant freshness, and contain much interesting information, and not a little old Athenian gossip, culled from Athenæus and elsewhere. The critical Appendix is most interesting. The reader will find a remarkably graphic sketch of the feeling in Greece at this time in Mr. Rogers's Preface. We anticipate with much pleasure the promise given in the Preface to this Play that we may shortly look for a version of the Thesmophoriazusæ from the same pen."—*London Review.*

"The best metrical version which we ever remember to have seen of any of the Plays of Aristophanes. We hope that so vigorous a translator and so genuine an admirer of Aristophanes will persevere in his undertaking. General readers will not easily find another translator who does his work with so much spirit and such evident enjoyment."—*Spectator.*

"A scholarly translation, so lively yet so literal as to console for the loss which literature sustains by the unfinished condition of Frere's treatment of the same Play."—*Saturday Review.*

"In a former translation by Mr. Rogers (as we said at the time), not only the meaning and metres of Aristophanes are faithfully represented, but also his tone and spirit: his sparkling wit, his pointed raillery, his broad farce, his poetical flights, and the manly vigour of his sober moods. The work now before us seems to have all the merits which distinguished Mr. Rogers's former performance as a translation, while as a piece of critical editing it is decidedly superior to it. If the Comedies of Aristophanes are to be naturalized in English, it would not be easy to find a translator more suited in every way for the task than Mr. Rogers has shown himself to be. Compared with Frere or Mitchell, he has greatly the advantage in terseness and compactness, preserving far more of the form of the original; and though of course such closeness cannot be attained without occasional loss of freedom and spirit, it is surprising to see how little is really sacrificed."—*Athenæum.*

"Mr. Rogers has translated the 'Peace' in a manner bespeaking an accomplished scholar. His aim is to be literal, but not at the expense of readableness, and the compromise is very cleverly carried into effect. Freedom as regards metre and expression is recognized within due bounds and under the surveillance of a correct ear and an unpedantic taste. The result is a very pleasing version. It entitles him to a rank not far below Walsh and Frere among first-class translators of Aristophanes."—*Contemporary Review.*

ALSO,

THE WASPS OF ARISTOPHANES.

ACTED AT ATHENS AT THE LENÆAN FESTIVAL, B.C. 422.

The Greek Text Revised, with a Translation into Corresponding Metres, and Original Notes. Small 4to.

"We recommend this volume to the reader as the most valuable and pleasant edition of a Greek play that we have ever met."—*British Quarterly.*

"It would be impossible to excel this admirable line-for-line translation. Mr. Rogers stands on equal grounds with Frere."—*New Quarterly.*

"Consists of text, notes, and translations: the text carefully revised in the light of that classical erudition which Mr. Rogers is known to possess, the translation done in a masterly style that may fairly be pronounced in the manner of Frere, and the notes full of learning and valuable illustration. No commendation could be too high for most of those portions of the translation done into long rhymed metres."—*London Quarterly.*

"All students of Aristophanes will feel grateful to Mr. Rogers. It is hardly too much to say that he has given a new value and interest to the play."—*Saturday Review.*

"As for the manner in which Mr. Rogers has done his work, it is difficult to use praise sufficiently high. His notes are full of excellent scholarship, and leave nothing to be desired in the way of explanation. As for his translation, it is simply a marvel of ease and skill. It would not be too much to say that no English translation of a classical author surpasses the rhymed portions."—*Spectator.*

"A delightful rendering of a famous play."—*Educational Times.*

"Decidedly the most complete edition as yet published in England. We earnestly hope that Mr. Rogers will not rest till he has given us the less known plays with equal completeness."—*Academy.*

"Mr. Rogers has a marvellous facility in metre and rhyme. In the translation, where all is excellent, it is difficult to select."—*Athenæum.*

"Quite equal to Frere, and somewhat closer to the original."—*Pictorial Times.*

"Mr. Rogers's success as a translator is so marked, we had almost said so brilliant, that we cannot but regret that he did not choose a play which would have afforded freer scope to his powers. Indeed, in his fertility of rhythmic resource, he may almost be said to rival the inexhaustible wealth of his original."—*Pall Mall Gazette.*

"A very careful, scholarly, and useful book."—*Journal of Education.*

"Excellently translated and edited."—*Evening Standard.*

"Acceptable alike to the scholar and the general reader."—*Press and St. James's Chronicle.*

"A clear and accurate text, a capital commentary, and, above all, undoubtedly the best verse translation of the play which has yet been published. By way of adding our quota to the chorus of praise which Mr. Rogers's 'Wasps' is eliciting, we need only say that it is his happiest effort."—*Examiner.*

www.ingramcontent.com/pod-product-compliance
Lightning Source LLC
Chambersburg PA
CBHW021642270326
41931CB00008B/1132